Popular PERFORMER

1920s & 1930s Love Songs

Arranged by MARY K. SALLEE

The Best Romantic Standards

The 1920s and 1930s have a stunning array of memorable and moving love songs. This collection revisits these great hits, casting them in the rich voice of the piano. The popular jazz standards "Stormy Weather" (1933) and "Somebody Loves Me" (1924) are represented along with songs that have been featured in movies—"Easy to Love" (*Born to Dance*) and "It Had to Be You" (*The Roaring Twenties; Casablanca; Annie Hall; When Harry Met Sally*)—and Broadway originals such as "Begin the Beguine" (*Jubilee*), "More Than You Know" (*Great Day*), and "Tea for Two" (*No, No, Nannette*). The bluesy swing of "I Only Have Eyes for You," the expansive melody of "Stardust," and all of the other wonderful musical moments are certain to provide hours of enjoyment for the pianist who wishes to be a *Popular Performer*.

CONTENTS

Cover image: United Artists/Photofest
© Caddo Company/United Artists

Copyright © MMIX by ALFRED PUBLISHING CO., INC.
All rights reserved.   Printed in USA.
ISBN-10: 0-7390-5676-X
ISBN-13: 978-0-7390-5676-9

BEGIN THE BEGUINE

Words and Music by Cole Porter
Arr. Mary K. Sallee

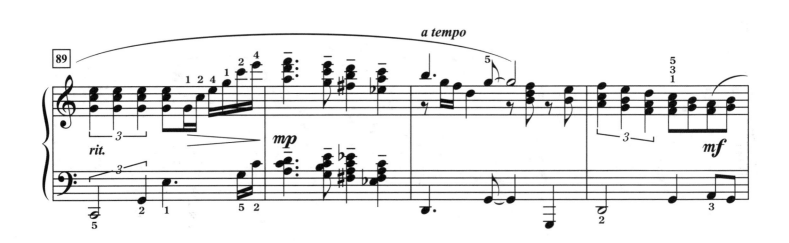

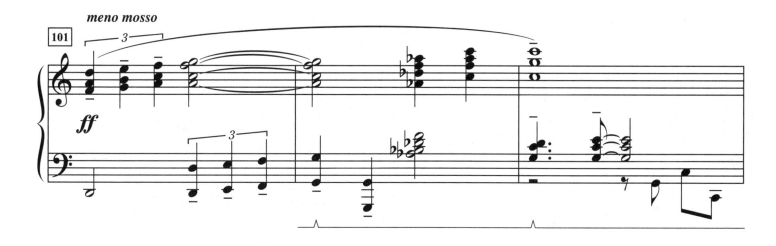

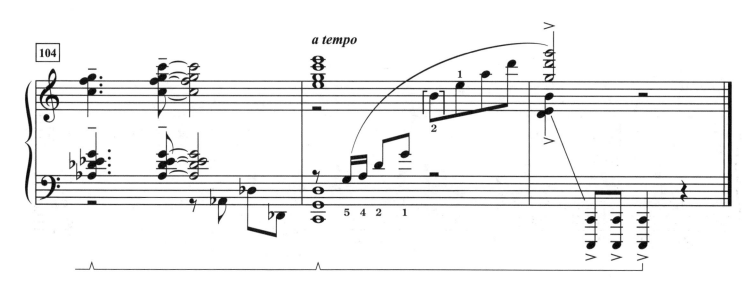

DREAM A LITTLE DREAM OF ME

Lyrics by Gus Kahn
Music by Fabian Andre and Wilbur Schwandt
Arr. Mary K. Sallee

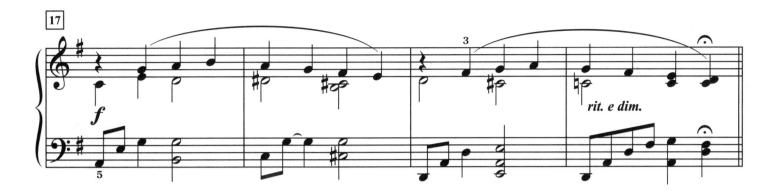

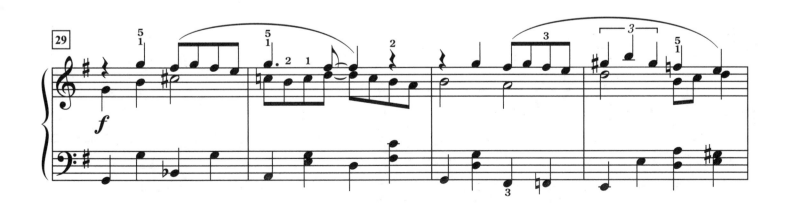

Easy to Love

Words and Music by Cole Porter
Arr. Mary K. Sallee

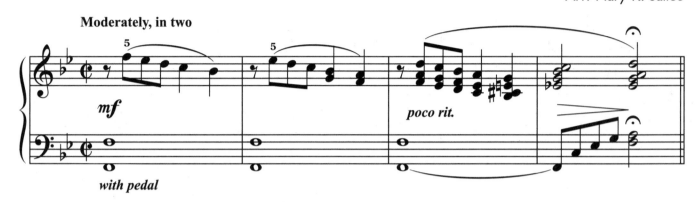

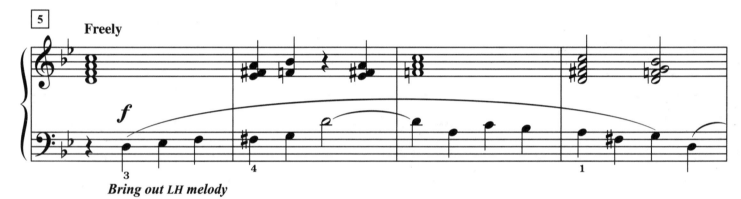

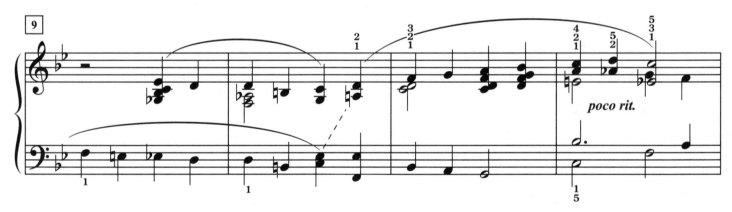

I Only Have Eyes for You

Words by Al Dubin
Music by Harry Warren
Arr. Mary K. Sallee

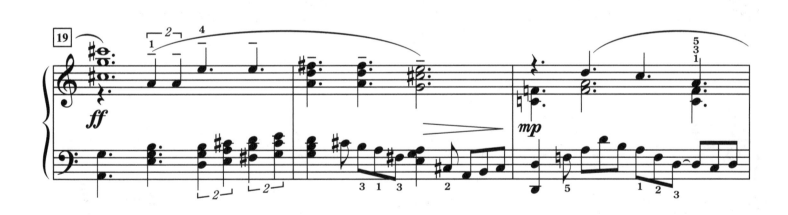

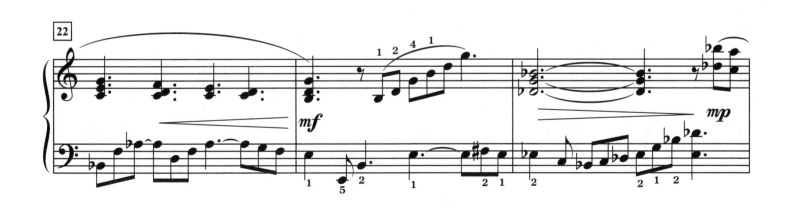

It Had to Be You

Words by Gus Kahn
Music by Isham Jones
Arr. Mary K. Sallee

More Than You Know

Words by William Rose and Edward Eliscu
Music by Vincent Youmans
Arr. Mary K. Sallee

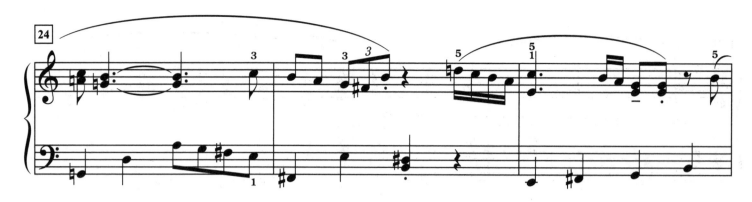

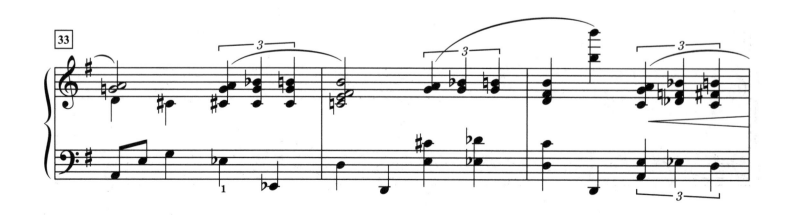

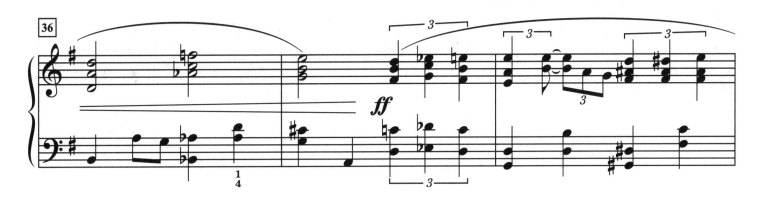

Somebody Loves Me

Music by George Gershwin
Lyrics by B.G. DeSylva and Ballard Macdonald
Arr. Mary K. Sallee

STORMY WEATHER

Words by Ted Koehler
Music by Harold Arlen
Arr. Mary K. Sallee

poco più mosso

Stardust

Music by Hoagy Carmichael
Words by Mitchell Parish
Arr. Mary K. Sallee

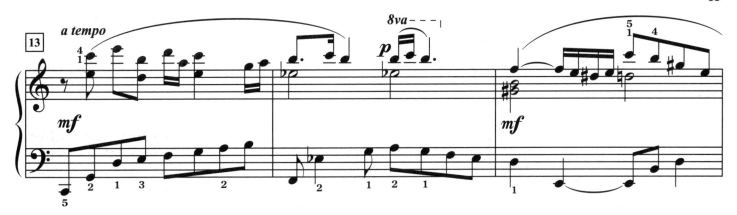

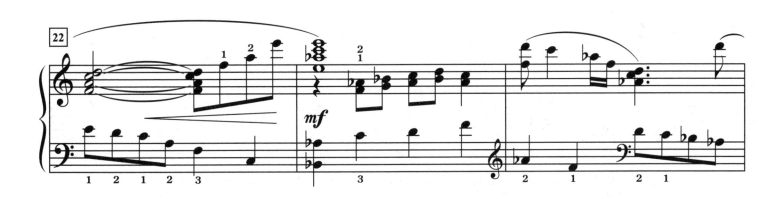

Tea for Two

Words by Irving Caesar
Music by Vincent Youmans
Arr. Mary K. Sallee

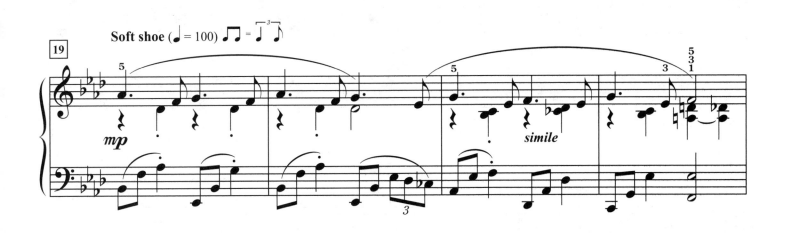

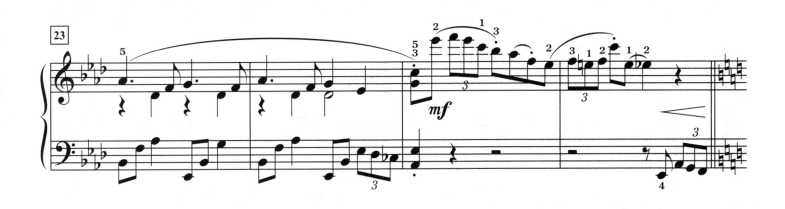